C000154188

יהוה

"

All scripture is given by inspiration of God, and is profitable for doctrine, for reproof, for correction, for instruction in rightousness. That the man of God may be perfect, throughly furnished into all good works.

"

2 TIMOTHY 3:16-17

יהוה

"

Christ bore my sins in His own body on the cross and I am healed by His stripes.

"

1 PETER 2:24

יהוה

"

*I speak God's Word
and hearing the Word
increases my faith.*

"

ROMANS 10:17

יהוה

"

*As I speak God's Word,
He sends it to heal and
deliver me from my
destruction.*

"

PSALM 107:20

יהוה

"

I speak words of life. I am satisfied with the good by the fruit produced by the words.

"

PROVERBS 12:14 / 18:20

יהוה

"

*I persist in speaking
God's Word until it
accomplishes its
purpose. It is like fire.
It is like a hammer that
shatters a rock.*

"

JEREMIAH 23:29

יהוה

"

I speak God's Word and His angels do the voice of His Word.

"

PSALM 103:20

יהוה

"

I declare God's Word about who I am, what I have, and what I can have in Christ Jesus who gives me strength. I am established as His daughter in all ways and I shine in his light.

"

JOB 22:8 / ISAIAH 60:1

יהוה

"

As I live in God, my love grows more perfect. I can face Him with confidence on the day of judgment because I live like Jesus here in this world.

"

1 JOHN 4:17 NLT

יהוה

"

I receive an abundance of grace and the gift of righteousness. I reign in life through Jesus Christ.

"

ROMANS 5:17

יהוה

"

I look out not only for my own interests but also for the interests of others.

"

PHILIPPIANS 2:4

יהוה

"

I am kind and tenderhearted to others. I forgive them as God in Christ has forgiven me.

"

EPHESIANS 4:32

יהוה

"

I can do all things through Christ who strengthens me.

One of Grandma's
favourite prayers.

"

PHILIPPIANS 4:13

יהוה

"

I ask God to set a guard over my mouth. He keeps watch over the door of my lips.

"

PSALM 141:3

יהוה

"

I let the Peace of Christ rule in my heart. As a member of one body, I am called to peace and I am thankful.

,,

COLOSSIANS 3:15

יהוה

"

*I walk in a manner
worthy of the Lord,
pleasing Him in all
respects. I bear fruit
in every good work and
I am increasing in the
knowledge of God.*

"

COLOSSIANS 1:10

יהוה

"

I am being strengthened with all power according to His might. I have great endurance and patience.

"

COLOSSIANS 1:11

יהוה

"

God has not given me a spirit of fear. He gives me power, love, and self-discipline

"

2 TIMOTHY 1:7

יהוה

"

God loads me daily with benefits. He is my salvation.

"

PSALM 68:19

יהוה

"

I am God's servant and He takes pleasure in my prosperity.

"

PSALM 35:27

יהוה

"

*God makes all grace
abound toward me so
that I always have all
sufficiency and an
abundance for every
good work.*

"

2 CORINTHIANS 9:8

יהוה

"

I honor the Lord with my wealth and the first fruits of all my produce. Then, my barns will be filled with plenty. My vats will overflow with new wine.

"

PROVERBS 3:9-10

יהוה

"

I bring the whole tithe into the storehouse. He opens the windows of heaven for me and pours out a blessing so great that I don't have enough room for it.

"

MALACHI 3:10

יהוה

"

I prosper in all things.
I remain in health just
as my soul prospers.

"

3 JOHN 1:3

יהוה

"

*God abundantly blesses
my provision.*

"

PSALM 132:15

יהוה

"

*I give and I receive.
Good measure, pressed
down, shaken together,
running over, will it be
put into my lap.*

"

LUKE 6:38

יהוה

"

*I give and I receive.
Good measure, pressed
down, shaken together,
running over, will it be
put into my lap.*

"

LUKE 6:38

יהוה

"

Jesus Christ is generous in grace. Though He was rich, yet for my sake he became poor, so that by His poverty He could make me rich.

"

2 CORINTHIANS 8:9

יהוה

"

Christ redeemed me from the curse of the law by becoming a curse for me.

"

GALATIONS 3:13

יהוה

"

I experience all blessings as I obey the Lord my God.

"

DEUTERONOMY 28:2

"

*I am blessed in the city
and blessed in the
country.*

"

DEUTERONOMY 28:3

יהוה

"

I am blessed from the fruit of my body. I am blessed with today's equivalent of the produce of the ground, the increase of my herds, my cattle, and the offspring of my flock.

"

DEUTERONOMY 28:4

יהוה

"

My kneading bowl and basket are blessed. It is the means by which I am tangibly increasing.

"

DEUTERONOMY 28:5

יהוה

"

I am blessed when I come in and blessed when I go out.

"

DEUTERONOMY 28:6

יהוה

"

The LORD causes my enemies who rise against me to be defeated before my face; they come out against me one way and flee before me seven ways.

"

DEUTERONOMY 28:7

יהוה

"

The LORD commands His blessing on my storehouses and in all that I set my hand to do, and He blesses me in the land that He is giving me.

"

DEUTERONOMY 28:8

יהוה

"

The Lord has established me as a holy person to Himself. I keep His commandments and walk in His ways.

"

DEUTERONOMY 28:9

יהוה

"

All the people of the
earth see that I am
called by the name of
the LORD.

"

DEUTERONOMY 28:10

יהוה

"

*The LORD grants me
plenty of goods, in the
fruit of my body, in the
increase of my
livestock, and in the
produce of my ground.*

"

DEUTERONOMY 28:11

יהוה

"

The LORD opens to me His good treasure, the heavens to give the rain to my land in its season and to bless all the work of my hand.

"

DEUTERONOMY 28:12

יהוה

"

I lend to many nations
but I will not borrow.

"

DEUTERONOMY 28:12

יהוה

"

The Lord makes me the head and not the tail, above and not beneath.

"

DEUTERONOMY 28:13

יהוה

"

*I am my Father's
daughter. I am always
with Him and all that
He has is mine.*

"

LUKE 15:31

יהוה

"

God blesses me and surrounds me with favour as a shield.

"

PSALM 5:12

יהוה

"

*My ways please the
LORD and He makes
even my enemies to be
at peace with me.*

"

PROVERBS 16:7

יהוה

"

But by God's doing I am in Christ Jesus. He became to me wisdom, righteousness, sanctification, and redemption.

"

1 CORINTHIANS 1:30

יהוה

"

*The God of hope fills
me with all joy and
peace in believing so
that I abound in hope
by the power of the
Holy Spirit.*

"

ROMANS 15:13

יהוה

"

The Lord of Peace is Peace. In every way, He always gives me His Peace.

"

2 THESSALONIANS 3:16

יהוה

"

I always rejoice and pray without ceasing. In everything, I give thanks for this is the will of God in Christ Jesus for me.

"

2 THESSALONIANS 5:16-18

יהוה

"

I am steadfast of mind.
He keeps me in perfect
Peace because I trust
in Him.

"

ISAIAH 26:3

יהוה

"

The joy of the LORD is my strength.

"

NEHEMIAH 8:10

יהוה

"

I am confident of this very thing, that He who has begun a good work in me will complete it until the day of Jesus Christ.

"

PHILIPPIANS 1:6

יהוה

"

God works in me both to will and to do His good pleasure.

"

PHILIPPIANS 2:13

יהוה

"

I do all things without grumbling or complaining so that I will prove myself to be blameless and innocent. I am a child of God who is above reproach in the midst of a crooked and perverse generation, among whom I appear as lights in the world,

"

PHILIPPIANS 2:14-15

יהוה

"

I hold fast to the word of life. In the day of Christ's return, I will have reason to glory because I did not run or labor in vain.

"

PHILIPPIANS 2:16

יהוה

"

I choose to meditate on anything that has virtue or is praiseworthy. I think about things are true, noble, just, pure, lovely, and of good report.

"

PHILIPPIANS 4:8

יהוה

"

I am anxious for nothing, but in everything by prayer and supplication with thanksgiving I let my requests be made known to God. And the Peace of God, which surpasses all comprehension, will guard my hearts and minds in Christ Jesus.

"

PHILIPPIANS 4:4-5

יהוה

"

I press on, that I may lay hold of that which Christ Jesus has also laid hold of me. Forgetting those things which are behind and reaching forward to those things which are ahead, I press toward the goal for the prize of the upward call of God in Christ Jesus.

"

PHILIPPIANS 3:12-14

יהוה

"

I always rejoice in the Lord and my gentleness is known to all people.

"

PHILIPPIANS 4:4-5

יהוה

"

The Lord is my God!
He is mighty to save.
He rejoices over me
with gladness and
singing. I am quieted
by His love.

"

ZEPHANIAH 3:17

יהוה

"

God instructs me and keeps me as the apple of His eye.

"

ZACHARIAH 2:8

יהוה

"

I am a crown of glory and a royal diadem in the hand of the LORD.

"

ISAIAH 62:3

יהוה

"

*I am no longer called,
Forsaken or Desolate.
My new names are
Hepbzibah (my delight
is in her) and Beulah
(married). He delights
in me and I am married
to Him.*

"

ISAIAH 62:4

יהוה

"

*God rejoices over me
as a bridegroom
rejoices over his bride.*

"

ISAIAH 62:5

יהוה

"

*The LORD has chosen
me for Himself as His
special treasure.*

"

PSALM 135:4

יהוה

"

I speak God's word and it does not return to Him void. His word accomplishes what He pleases and it prospers in the thing for which He sends it.

"

ISAIAH 55:11

יהוה

"

The Lord has given me the tongue of the disciples. I know how to speak a word in due season to those who are weary.

"

ISAIAH 50:4

יהוה

"

The Lord God awakens me every morning to fellowship with Him, and He opens my ears to hear as the learned.

"

ISAIAH 50:4

יהוה

"

I speak pleasant words that are sweet to the soul and healing to the bones. I am wise and I bring healing.

"

PROVERBS 16:24 / 12:18

יהוה

I have a wholesome tongue which is a tree of life to myself and others.

PROVERBS 15:4 / 11:30 / 18:21

יהוה

"

God forgives all my iniquities and heals all of my diseases.

"

PSALM 103:3

יהוה

"

God redeems my life from the pit. He crowns me with lovingkindness and compassion.

"

PSALM 103:4

יהוה

"

*God satisfies my mouth
with good things and
renews my youth like
the eagles'.*

"

PSALM 103:5

יהוה

"

Thank you
&
God Bless You :)

"

DEBORAH RAITER

Printed in Great Britain
by Amazon

40833129R00066